THE
LITTLE
BOOK
— ABOUT —
GOD

Lauren Ford

Doubleday & Company, Inc.
Garden City, New York

Library of Congress Cataloging in Publication Data

Ford, Lauren, 1891–1973
   The little book about God.

   Previous ed.: Doubleday, Doran, 1934.
   Summary: Retells well-known Bible stories including
the story of the Creation, Noah and his ark, and the
birth of Christ.
   1. Bible stories, English. [1. Bible stories]
I. Title.
BS551.F57 1985   220.9'505   81-43749
ISBN 0-385-17691-0   AACR2

9 8 7 6 5 4 3 2

To Lauren ~~
from
Grandma ~~

Once upon a time the whole world was called B.C. and now it is called A.D. and this is a story to tell you why and how and all about it.

Now long, long ago God
was up in Heaven and He
said, "It is time to begin
making the Earth"; so He
did. It was all plain Earth,
and He said, "That isn't
very interesting". So He
began to make a pattern
on it with   seas and
rivers   and hills
and   north
poles   and

every sort of thing that
doesn't grow any
bigger. Then He
put trees and
buttercups on,
and grass and pussy
willows, and all the
growing things that have
their feet inside the
ground
"There", He said
"that looks very
much better.
But I should
like so much to see
some things that can
move   about
on it."

Then God created ∽
lions for the Jungle and
little donkeys for the hills,
and goats and cows and
baby lambs and bunny
rabbits, and fishes for
the rivers, and ducks, too,
and   all the birds ℘ snakes
        and butterflies
    and   all the

Creatures of the Earth ,
and then He created people.

After God had worked
hard all week long to
make all these things it
was Sunday, so He took
a good long rest.

First God created
Adam; He put him
in a lovely garden all full
of good things to eat, and
where he could play all day.
"Only," God said,"you must
never eat the fruit of the,
tree of knowledge because
if you do you will surely
die", But Adam was
lonely   so God
created Eve.   Now
one day while Eve   was
talking to a snake   the
Spirit of Evil got   into the
snake, and he said"You had
better eat of the fruit of the
                tree   of
         knowledge

God said it would make you die, but it won't, it will only make you as wise as He is, and He wouldn't like that at all". So Eve did, and she gave some to Adam and he ate it too; and that is how the trouble began.

So God came down, and He said:" Now you are so wise, you must work for your livings; and all your children and grandchildren will have to go to work for ever and ever -

and I won't help you not to be nasty and mean to each other, but let you all alone to fight each other, and be as bad as you like.

So the people went away from the garden and began to be very busy.

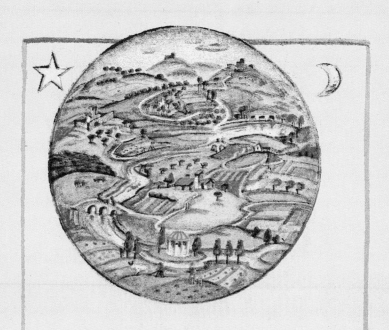

At first they didn't
change the pattern of
the things on the Earth
so very much, because
they only picked
apples and wild
strawberries.

They lived in caves and
fished in rivers,
and when they wanted
to take a bath they
went in swimming, and
they only knew their
very nearest neighbors.

But soon they had to learn
to do a great many
more things. When they
finished eating all the
strawberries that
grew near their caves

They had to go much farther away to get food. So they made roads. It was hot sometimes, so they planted trees along the roads to protect them from wind and sun and made bridges to cross the rivers on, & signposts to know which road to take for home.

Soon the people began to tame the animals. The dog came all by him-self to be a friend, and the donkey carried the sacks of nuts and berries, and the horse carried the people. Then they made coats out of the lamb's woolly covering and milked the cows and made fences to keep them near.

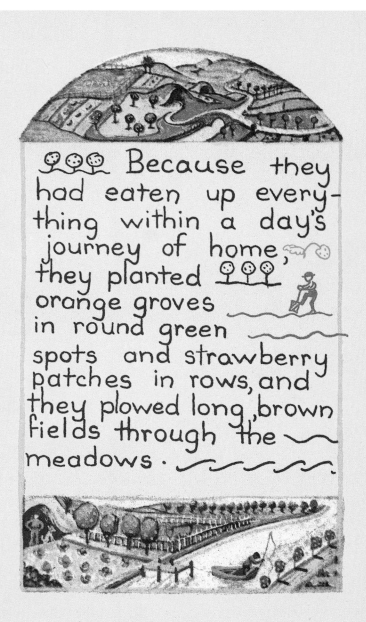

Because they had eaten up everything within a day's journey of home, they planted orange groves in round green spots and strawberry patches in rows, and they plowed long, brown fields through the meadows.

Then somebody discovered how to build a house, and of course everyone had to have one too, and that

is the way that towns began. Now all these new things changed the pattern on the Earth, and it was lovely to behold.

But the people could
not enjoy what they
had made.

They spoiled it with
war and dishonor
and pestilence and
famine and misery and
plain stupidity, and
this is the part of
the story that is all
about these horrid words

Now there were on Earth some people who were stupid, and some who were lazy. The stupid people couldn't learn to do anything; they couldn't plant a field, and they couldn't build a house, and they couldn't be of any use to themselves. And some hired themselves out to other people, and some just sat around, and others begged.

One day, when the stupid
people were on their
way to the fair to beg,
they met the lazy people.
And the lazy people said,
"Whenever you try to make
a thing you spoil it, and
whenever we try to
make a thing we go to
sleep. So let us take
all the things the
good people have."
So they
did.

Now the name they gave
to that was theft.

So the
people

built their houses inside
walls on the tops of the
hills, and at night they
took their beasts inside
and for a while that
worked.

Then the lazy people
said to the stupid people,
"We will get horses
and will make a mighty
army, and we will
pillage and burn the
towns."

So they did that thing.

And the name they
gave to it was war.

God said:"What is this
I see?"and He sent
the Angel Gabriel to inves-
tigate.

When the Angel
Gabriel came back
to Heaven he told God and
he said: "The people and
the animals are hurting
each other and the Earth
too", and God said "They are
very naughty indeed", and,
"I am so sorry for them,
even if they did eat the
fruit of the tree of
knowledge". Then He and the
Angel Gabriel worked hard to
save   the   Earth
and   people
and   the little

beasts from themselves. xxx.

He moved the
armies about from one
place to another, and He
made thunder and ⚡
lightning to keep the
wrong ones out, and
He made snow and hail
and rain to send them
back to their own
homes.

God made a great flood so that everything should start out all fresh and clean again. Now when the flood came God said to Mr. and Mrs. Noah, who were very good, "You will get in a boat and take a lady and a gentleman animal of every kind."

So they  did:

Then Mr. and Mrs. Noah and their children and the animals sailed and sailed in the rain. At last it cleared up nicely; so they let out their dove and back he flew ~~~ with an olive branch in his mouth – so they let the other birds fly – and then they saw a mountain. They all got out. But somehow the badness broke out all over again.

And God said, "I have had enough", and He said, "I will not have the Guardian Angels weeping all over Heaven", and He went into His garden.

While God was sitting in His
garden very quietly, He
began to hear a sound
coming up from His Earth
and the sound was like the
buzzing of a great
far-away bee.

And God became very interested ·/·/· And He began to listen, and separate it, one sound from another, and to find the place that each came from. First He listened to a great battle and then to the music where some people were dancing.

Then He listened to the cows munching their dinner and to the roar of the ocean

and to the little
birds singing in the
high trees, and to storms
in the wild dark forests,
and to the
lions
roaring
in the
tall grass, and to
baby lambs calling
to their
mummys
in the valleys.
And the sounds of
the Earth were very
interesting
to God.

And He said
"I do so
love My
Earth."
He went on listening.
He listened to men sing-
ing as they worked the
fields, and to a band of
children playing ring-
around-a-rosy.
   And while God
was hearing all
these sounds
and looking up each one
in its own place, He
heard one small high
sound that called through
and over all the others.

And God tried to find out what was this weeny sound, but it was hard to find. At last. He found it, and He rose up, and He called loud to the Angel Gabriel, and He said:

"This will never do".

And the Angel Gabriel said:

"What will never do?"

And the Lord God said: "Look into the kitchen of the house in the town where the stupid and lazy people have just finished making a war, and where all the people had to run away."

And the Angel Gabriel
looked, and He saw a little
girl crying at a table.
And there was no cereal
in the bowl. And there
was no bread on the plate.
And there was no mummy
in the other chair. And
there was no milk in the
milk bottle. And God said
to the Angel Gabriel:
"something must be done
about this immediately".

So the Angel Gabriel
flew very fast, and he
came to Earth, and he
took some of the milk
that was all fixed for
the Queen to take her
bath in.

And the
Angel
Gabriel
went to
the
house
of the
little girl, and he built
up the fire, and he warmed
the good milk, and he
prepared some cereal for
her, and when she had eat-
en he sang her
to sleep.

And he carried
the little girl to
the place
that

her
and
daddy
fled   to
because of
war.   And he gave her
to her mummy.

mummy
her
had

the

And the Angel Gabriel
came back to God, and
he said: "Surely we can
show these poor people
how to behave
to each
other,

they   are very
nice   when they
are   little."

Then   God said:
"If My   first
people had not disobeyed
Me about that fruit there
would be no lazy and
no stupid people."

And He said:

"Now I must save them,
for they have invented
suffering, and neither you
nor I can teach them, for
We can not suffer with
them. If We cut Our
finger it does not hurt
and if We have nothing
to eat We do not mind.

So I shall send My Son
to be born of one of
them. And He shall
grow up among them.
And He shall teach them
to love one another and to
love and to talk to Me
so that they can not be
nasty or bad any longer."

And God
said:

"There is a little girl on Earth, and when she is big she will be the Mother of My little Son because she is all good and happy."

And the little girl grew up.

At that time the Angel Gabriel was sent from God into a city of Galilee called Nazareth to the little girl, who was all grown up, and her name was Mary; and the Angel Gabriel being come in said unto her:

"Hail, full of Grace, the Lord
is with thee! Blessed art
thou amongst women.
Thou shalt have a Baby
Boy, and He shall be called
the Son of the Most High"

and Mary was very glad.

Now one day Mary and Joseph went to Bethlehem, and there was no more room in the inn. So they went into the stable, and the Baby Boy was born, and they laid Him in a manger. And there were in that country shepherds abiding in the fields, keeping watch over their flocks by night. And the Angel of the Lord stood near them, and the glory of the Lord shone round about them, and they were sore afraid.

And the Angel said to them: "Fear not, for behold I bring you good tidings of great joy, that shall be to all people; for this day is born to you a Saviour who is Christ the Lord. And this shall be a sign unto you: You shall find the Infant wrapped in swaddling clothes and laid in a manger. And suddenly there was with the Angel a multitude of the Heavenly army praising God and saying: "Glory to God in the Highest; and on Earth Peace."

And this was the
First Christmas of all

Now everything before
this was called B.C. ～～
which means before Christ,
and everything now is ～
called A.D.= In the year
of Our Lord. And if you
are hungry your mummy
gives you some good ～
supper — Because Our ～
Lord is born to teach us
all about kindness. ～～